FINDING FREEDOM

Through Art Therapy

and Writing

Margaret Braim Little

Written and Illustrated by: Margaret Braim Little

First Edition

Cover design and all photos in book are original paintings of Margaret Little
Typeset at Spica book design (www.spicabookdesign.com)

FSC

Printed and bound in Canada by Island Blue Book Printing, Victoria B.C.
(www.islandblue.com)

Typesetting by Darcy Nybo, Artistic Warrior Publishing
and Roseanna White Designs

ISBN: 978-1-7773564-0-8

I would like to dedicate this book to all children and to all who are courageously trying to make sense of their lives. I hope that this book will encourage understanding that the way we act and talk to others has a potent affect, especially on our children and "The Child's Gift" that each one brings to earth.

May Love and Peace come to all on Earth

Table of Contents

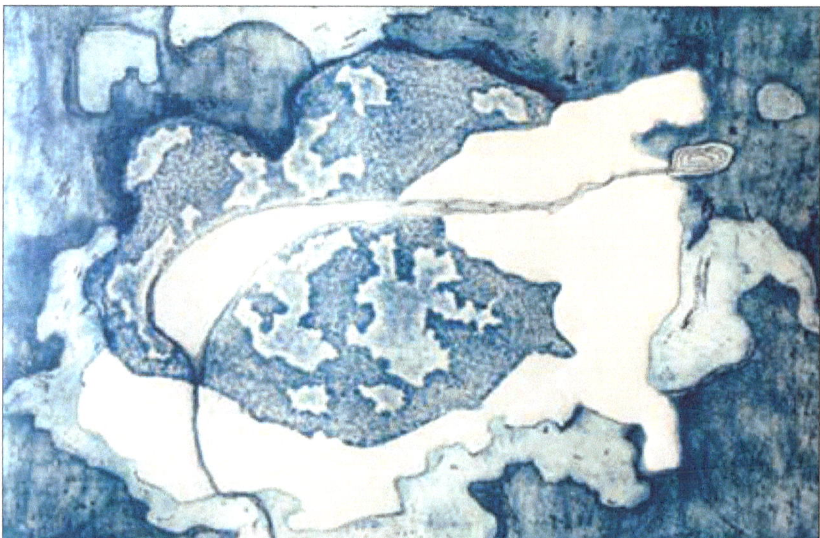

The Universe

Foreword

For two years, I met weekly with Margaret in psychotherapy sessions as she struggled to find life again after a torn marriage and painful divorce.

At first, she was deeply depressed as she struggled with herself to find the words to express the depth of her painful personal story. Antidepressant pills were not solving her problems, and neither was talk therapy. She was stuck.

But Margaret was also a visual artist. Her talent and skill shone through in her pictures of flowers, landscapes and her abstracts. Somehow, despite her troubles and darkness, she was able to express beauty through pigments and brushes. Might this talent for expression also be harnessed to become a way of dancing with her emotions until they became digested and transformed? Could she employ the tools with which she created beauty for metabolizing the pain of her past and present, and growing beyond that pain? Could her art become her therapy?

I began to encourage Margaret to express her personal story – her pain and despair, yes, but also her love and her hope - through her art. Again she struggled, but Margaret was perseverant. She began to shed her need to produce aesthetic, "fine art", and started to trust her art to speak her raw, honest personal *truth*. Her paintings record her adventures in emotional authenticity.

Margaret found the courage to put herself out on paper, where she can be seen. She took the risks always involved in revealing her images to herself as well as others. But her journey was rewarded. Her expressions of sadness, anger, loneliness or despair also opened up new vistas within her, new possibilities, new grounds for hope. And old ground to be reclaimed. Through her paintings, Margaret began to weave the shreds of her past life into a new fabric of personal meaning she could trust.

Margaret's art became her way of *showing* what could not be fully told. Her paintings tilled her inner ground more deeply than her words could reach. Through these images, she found her *visual* voice, and in using that voice she began to find herself, to find love for herself, and to remake her life. Margaret came to understand that there are no truly intolerable *events*, only intolerable *stories*. She found that in becoming restored, she was also becoming re*storied*. Through her picture-making journey, she began to tell a new story of a way forward.

We don't have all of Margaret's pictures. She didn't keep every painting she made. Sometimes, her journey forward lay in letting go of images of the past. Her letting go of those images was just as important to her healing and growth as was the keeping of others.

In her paintings, Margaret found her measure of peace. She gave me a parting gift – an etching titled 'Universe' that hung for years in my Brentwood BC office. It shows me Margaret's endless change … around her deep core of eternality.

Bruce Tobin, Ph.D.
November, 2020

Preface

There was originally no intention to write a book. The breakup of my marriage precipitated many events. This story is about some life changes and survival discovered and created through art.

Write a book? I had just spent several years with an art therapist helping me recover from the pain of separation and divorce. Writing a book was not in my consciousness.

My husband and I had, approximately one year earlier, retired to an island off the west coast of Canada. During the construction of an addition to a rundown cottage, my husband left. After living in a marriage relationship for almost 40 years, here I was just six months short of 60 years of age, alone.

Although I had many friends who supported me emotionally, it was up to me to recreate myself. I was the only person who could do it, but I needed help.

At that time, I attended an art-therapy, two-day conference and workshop. When I read the names, there was only one session I really wanted. I attended it, discovered the leader was giving an evening course at a university in a nearby city and immediately signed up for it. Although I had to travel by ferry and stay overnight, I knew there was hope for me by taking this direction. Thus, I actively took actions towards reclaiming my life. Working with the psychologist I was drawn to, has proved to be incalculably positive and necessary.

But, one morning before dawn, I wakened with a dream: words spilling through my mind. They were so clear; I was certain

I would remember each one. A second thought suggested I might forget. I then struggled half awake, picked up my nearby notebook, and began penciling those outpourings. At first, I couldn't find or express enough words. Speaking words was always a challenge, and I tended to be quiet in groups. Therefore, my vocabulary hadn't developed any great variety through the years. The writing moved slowly and included a tone of depression.

Upon completion, I read and edited the work. Satisfied, I lay back and returned to sleep. As this was obviously not going to happen, I reluctantly sat up, reread what I'd written, removed the editing and found a five-hundred-word introduction to a book.

"Oh my!" was my reaction. I thought I had already clearly expressed my emotions regarding our split relationship. My conditioning by family and society had been explored. Psychological reactions and philosophical ideas were detailed. All this was recorded in my series of acrylic paintings created over several years. Early pictures expressed emotions. Later paintings developed around themes. Now it appeared that perhaps my process was not complete

Throughout, I had a constant internal director strongly urging me forward to delve inward to depths I didn't know, or even imagine, existed. I also required and took spaces of time of several days or longer, leaving painting and dealing with many surfacing emotions.

I scoured through accumulated past experiences. During this time of research, I experienced a wide range of emotions.

But I have completed what I needed to do and can appreciate my life and what I have learned. I am very grateful that I had the strength and persistence to carry forward this exploration.

At one point during my therapy, I was overcome with the need to burn all the paintings so carefully created during the revelatory work I had done. When that urge to burn them arrived, I stopped, realizing slides and snapshots that had been taken at various times were available. They were not as detailed or as accurate as I would now have wanted them to be. I found that once I began to use words, emotions and thoughts were expressed in more detail, clearing out inner resistances. It was further catharsis and a fuller picture emerged.

After setting my manuscript aside for a few years I became aware that passing time had presented a new awareness. I had included patterns occurring in my family and discovered that some were carried in me. Reflections of influences of societies conditioning had evolved into fuller considerations of many aspects of my life.

To portray immediacy, I used present tense to describe the actual and emotional processes of the development of a painting. Past tense seemed best for historical sections and afterthoughts, some of which arrived several years later.

Endeavoring to give honest and open expression, my vulnerability was exposed. I developed more humanness and saw that wearing masks or building psychological walls, either for denial or supposed security, could prevent true personal connection and compassion.

Although I wrote about myself, the story relates to the lives of many others. The importance of allowing and assisting children to develop their innate individual talents is clearly illustrated. By understanding human behaviour more clearly, freedom follows to accept and encourage all children in fulfilling their talents on their individual journeys.

Now, years later, an Epilogue is written and includes many additional awarenesses. The original information regarding the process of the paintings remains but is told with increased clarity. Hopefully some information here may encourage others to explore a deeper understanding of their journey. In particular I desire that there is even greater recognition of the importance of children's early experiences and an increased desire to assist them to reach their full potential.

Introduction

This book is a unique offering of the journey of one woman working through a process of seeking and finding freedom through art as therapy and writing this book as an expression of that story of discovery. My husband of 37 years had just left, soon after having moved us from a city social life to a small rural coastal island. As an artist and almost sixty, I was confused, in shock. I was unable to pick up a paintbrush or do any artwork. During the following 3 years, layers and perspectives surfaced in these paintings concerning myself as a child, a married woman with family and finally a newly single person looking for her true self and direction. Slowly, over time, and encouraged by an art therapy psychologist, I slowly returned to creating.

Wakening one morning with a dream, I quickly wrote down the message reeling forth. At this time I had no inclination to write a book. Twenty-five coloured illustrations of acrylic paintings, some abstract, and others life size individual and group portraitures, became the basis for discussion in this story of will and determination to understand my life. Writing was a further catharsis for healing my heart and parts of my inner child. Psychological and philosophical considerations regarding ancestral streams of consciousness and human life weave throughout this first person tale. This art therapy memoir tells an in-depth, honest, open and experiential narrative of psychological understanding of one woman's life, her family heritage, and of wisdom about humanness. It discusses the importance of childhood experiences and other events and how they affected and informed her life. This story may have relevance for other individuals in their own understanding of relationships and life journey.

1. An Impulse, a Dilemma

I wanted to burn all my paintings created during the past three-and-one-half years. Holding me back was the question, "If I keep the paintings, can they help others?"

What led to this impulse? Was it that last visit with my psychologist? Was it my feelings when I burned one of my paintings three days ago? Was it the talk recently with one of my daughters, who expressed her understanding now of herself, her dad and me? Or is it simply a point I have reached in my healing process?

As usual, I begin near the end of my story. I even read newspapers commencing with the front page and then read the back page and continue from that point and move towards the front. So, let me go to . . . I was going to say, the beginning, but who actually knows where anything really begins?

I'll start at the point when my husband of almost thirty-five years decided to end our marriage. I was six months short of sixty years and he was fifty-seven years old. Why was this event so catastrophic? Someone my age would likely understand, but comprehension by younger generations, now so adapted to one, two, or even three divorces, might find it difficult to comprehend. Our generation was expected to remain married until death parted us, and to be divorced was scandalous.

My husband had taken early retirement and we moved to a small island off the coast of British Columbia. He had some difficulty adjusting and missed his university support team. He continued consulting with business firms. Just over a year after our relocation, on the morning of December third, he permanently left.

In retrospect, I realized the closeness of our relationship had been collapsing for several years. Neither of us understood what the other needed, or even what we needed for ourselves, and this was combined with our difficulty to communicate clearly. Also, I held the belief it was important to remain together as parents to our daughters. It is now clear to me that it is more important for children to be in a loving and calm environment rather than one of tension. Pain piled up inside. Finally, frustration and anger due to unmet needs caused the elastic band to snap.

As a result of the parting, I slipped into major depression. I felt guilt and shame that I'd failed to obtain the dream of lasting marriage. Despair and anger arrived when he was unwilling to have a discussion of our issues with me; instead, he wanted a younger woman. I judged myself inadequate in dealing with the situation and developed a great self- questioning about my life and situation.

My hope had been that our change of location and lifestyle meant a chance for us to again relate closely because there would be additional time to explore and enjoy activities together. This illusion was dashed. We had moved from the world of professors and dinner parties, new subdivisions and municipal services to an isolated rural island community. The language of wells and septic fields was as alien as another planet for me. I didn't know simple things such as a major electrical failure meant that toilets wouldn't flush because the well pump wouldn't start.

As had many women my age, I had worked for a short period in the 1950s and then married, centering attention on my family and their activities. I had not lived on my own and had only managed my own money before marriage for about two years. My career and sense of worth as a homemaker had now disappeared and my primary desire was to run away from everything and everyone to someplace totally new and different. But I soon realized my emotions would remain present. I was disoriented and felt downhearted and alone.

Creating art works had been a constant interest since my early childhood. I began winning awards, the first at ten years of age, and although none were grand awards, they encouraged me to continue. I had completed many art courses, been invited into exhibition and sales, and taken part in a few art shows. Several years before my husband left, I had mounted a solo art show. Now I found it impossible to pick up an art paintbrush or do any other artwork. That inability was a serious indication of my loss of a feeling for life itself.

Making choices was difficult and I had no idea what I wanted to do with my life. Most seriously, I did not know who I was as a separate identity. I was in shock and clearly aware that something had to change. I needed help understanding myself.

As the following autumn drew near, I read about an art therapy conference in Vancouver, BC. The only name attracting me turned out to be a university art therapy psychologist. During his workshop I heard he would be leading art therapy sessions for ten weeks in Victoria, BC, and I immediately signed up. This meant traveling by ferry for each class and staying at a Bed and Breakfast overnight. A few months later, feeling I was not making much progress in regaining a sense of myself, I began individual counseling with this psychologist. His office was opposite a cottage enclosed by a fence covered with particularly beautiful roses. I had previously driven out of my way to pass this hedge when returning from the city on my way home. Considering this coincidence, I wondered if I had subconsciously known what might be lying ahead for me.

Encouraged by the art therapist, my painting impasse finally broke and I began to express myself freely and spontaneously with poster paint on newsprint.

My upbringing included a general attitude that children should be seen and not heard. Old tapes about acting properly coiled around inside. The hurt was too severe and I had been programmed to not admit to having, let alone speak about or show, such thoughts to an observer. My anger frightened me. I was well trained to withhold passions and words. My upbringing included a lot of sayings like: "act properly," "don't be cheeky," and "children should be seen and not heard." When I finally verbalized emotions, it was often expressed with pent up force, occasionally accompanied with tears. I had never learned to assert myself clearly. Due to my previous experience as a painter, I was encouraged to allow acknowledgement of these feelings with paint.

The pictures in this book contain a story and are part of my search to answer inner questions. Why has this happened? What were the causes? Why did they develop? These paintings assisted me to better understand influencing factors in my life. They displayed my sentiments like a mirror. When a few trusted individuals saw the completed canvases, I found each of these friends choosing one or two favourites and each person selected differently. I noticed that what was inside me, and now in the pictures, was acting as a reflection of hidden emotions in the other person. Because I knew what my picture expressed, I could better understand the viewer. Therefore, a dilemma arose about my desire to burn the paintings and the risk of taking this action. Did they have another meaning or use, other than simply bringing out my inner emotions?

Now, relating the events of these years of painting while grieving my sense of loss, I realize that much information contained here is relevant to me and to the human family. This is not just my story.

2. Painting Again

My recovery begins with an art therapist. I casually illustrate scenes of my life and at other times simply throw poster paint onto inexpensive and disposable newsprint paper. Without pressure to produce results, I can allow a darker part of myself, buried deeply inside, to safely drip out to become acknowledged, honoured and regarded as legitimate.

The time arrives for me to progress and use artist's stretched canvas on wooden frames. Sheer fright causes me to gag when facing the white, blank space and my body resists and blocks any expression. Swirling thoughts develop questions. Can I still paint? Can I create something meaningful? In my belief system, a painting isn't just a pretty decoration to hang above or beside a chair to give matching or contrasting colours to the room. It has a deeper purpose to its shapes and design. Any picture, created in various ways and using diversified techniques, is a vehicle to express one or more of my innermost values, experiences or ideas. Alive with energy, it can elicit a responding human feeling and communicate an inner vision or message to the viewer. This is not always an easy task because my artwork also needs to have simplicity and clarity.

Entering my studio, I place in front of me a 24" x 24" primed canvas, jars of paints ready to be opened, and a selection of brushes of assorted sizes standing in a bottle. Finally, I pick up a medium sized brush, mix a turquoise colour and make a few strokes from the top edge downwards.

Fig. 1 Sadness Becoming Depression

Thinking about the separation and break-up of the relationship I feel extremely sad. I begin my first painting in several years. Then I spread purple around in a sort of figure eight. Standing back from the painting, I see one unlike any I've done previously. A few strokes on a white background create suggested movement and the image is so simple, I think it's incomplete. The critic in my head begins telling me how a painting should look and I fill the background with yellow, perhaps to suggest light around my darkness.

For the next couple of days, additional turquoise and purple redefine and change the areas.

I'm happy that I've returned to creating a work of *art*. As the colours become overworked, my frustration increases when I see the original clarity of sadness lost in the newly complex and obscured expression. I slip into dejection. I title the painting *Sadness Becoming Depression*. (Figure 1)

Suddenly, an inside spark moves me to pick up a second 24" x 24" canvas and complete a new picture in twenty minutes. This immediate impulse, expressed with definite quickly moving brushstrokes, creates an incomplete black circle with red outside. An additional red circle is painted inside and flashes out. A gold starburst flies in from outside. The black circle I interpret as my heavy heartedness. Upon completion of this painting, I no longer feel despondent and am aware of joy orbiting quietly around me. This painting is named *Edge of Anger*. (Figure 2)

Gazing at these two paintings, I realize there exist unexpressed, masked feelings. What is hidden? Is it unmet expectations? Is it a lack of self-worth? I wonder what the red symbolizes. Why do I rework the process? This type of continuous action seems to correlate with my need to use too many words, or excuses, in order to explain my feelings or actions.

Fig. 2 Edge of Anger

What truth is obscured? It is an old habit for me to keep reorganizing details in order to achieve what I intellectually perceive as perfection. Obviously, my mind circles through a wide variety of thoughts when I don't have a clear idea or direction. I decide it's enough surmising for now. I would like to reclaim the original painting of turquoise and purple.

It takes experience to know and to stop at the magic minute of completeness. This moment compares to an instant of silence: a period of doing nothing except waiting quietly. It resembles the stillness between two breaths. This is the place where there is no time and wisdom emerges. A solution to a situation feels right and brings inner calm.

As days pass, life carries on. I'm not certain, but perhaps painting will release my feeling of heaviness. Entering the studio, I pick up a slightly larger 24" x 30" canvas. Selecting red paint and focusing on my inner coil of pressure, I very slowly extend the tension into my brush held at arms-length. Firmly, I drag and push the colour onto the canvas until my brush hesitates and then bursts quickly free at the outer edge. Next an outside circle of black paint represents a protective enclosure and an added golden colour illustrates hope.

I find it incredible that this amount of stress can be released through brush strokes. The canvas now contains this emotion and is titled *Coiled Tension*. (Figure 3)

Tuning into my body, I sense a remaining tautness still held tightly in my diaphragm. Taking some deep breaths, I begin to relax and although now calmer, I feel more alive. My normal tendency is to take shallow breaths. Sometimes at night I suddenly waken, needing to breathe. Perhaps by consciously breathing, continued relaxation will be achieved. I am not yet seeing the joy in being able to create again.

Fig. 3 Coiled Tension

There is only a dim awareness that I have broken through an inner barrier to painting and now have three completed canvases. These last two attempts indicate value in allowing any expression to simply evolve, developing clarity, without expectations of how a painting should look.

It is not difficult to return to this feeling as I presently live in a pervasive sadness. Because a painting cannot be duplicated and still retain its life, I choose a new theme of a drapery. On another 24" x 24" canvas, vertical areas of pink and purple express suspended veils forming a curtain of sadness. For an unexplained reason, a white circle remains.

One day I pick up a small sculpture, a simple seated figure from Ecuador. I love holding and caressing its wood. This is the image I decide to place in the circle and gently brush it there. Golden light is pulled from the top corner into the solar plexus of the sculpture. I name the painting, *Sadness*. (Figure 4)

Perplexed by the white circle and contents, I wonder what they mean? Inspecting quietly, I speculate that the sculpture may represent part of the past and good memories. The gold colour brings in the Light of Spirit. The sculpture symbolizing the past and the light symbolizing the possible future, are my current points of reference and concentration. Many of my usual daily thoughts are of "what was" or of "what could be". Regrets, wishes or desires overwhelm me unless I focus on the present moment. My longing for space and peace seem very inaccessible. Taking some deep breaths and focusing on immediate activity with acceptance and enjoyment of what is occurring at the time can relax tension and allow increased inner freedom.

Over time I have acquired additional impressions about these paintings. The clear lines and colour of *Sadness becoming Depression* embodied sadness when I painted authentically in the present moment.

Fig. 4 Sadness

However, old restrictive thoughts controlled and blocked me, telling me that honest expression was not sufficient. Therefore, I repainted and hid the clarity. Inhibitions, not me, controlled my life.

Edge of Anger arose from feelings of despair. Painting quickly, I felt increased energy. But lurking in the shadows I discovered unacknowledged anger at my husband's manner of leaving. Continuing this inner search, additional sensations arose: disappointment about the separation as well as loneliness and a feeling of uselessness because I had been, in effect, fired from my job. It was important to then sit quietly until I unearthed other underlying feelings of sadness and frustration about a lack of communication.

Coiled Tension illustrated an added sense of how qualities of energy flow from us into whatever we are doing in our lives. Unexpressed feelings build body tension, but these can be transformed and released through physical activity. A reverse assumption could be that emotions stuck inside can create physical illness. Therefore, whatever is in our inner worlds, and in oudr subtle fields determines our outer expression of well-being or dis-ease.

What is in our heart and our mind is transmitted into our actions, our reactions, our work and our associations in the outer world. Also, one's energy and temperament affects, and is reflected, in any creative work whether it be music, painting, sculpture, writing or an organization. The paintings we hang on our walls influence us, knowingly and unknowingly, depending on the personal qualities of the painter. If what we live amongst in our environment impacts us, it is certainly desirable to choose carefully everything in our surroundings. It's even more important to be attentive to those individuals retained as friends and associates.

This is a profound realization.

Sadness was an effort to redo my first painting called *Sadness Becoming Depression.*

When I created this first picture, I hadn't understood I had become depressed, even though I subconsciously used the word in the title. I was dwelling on the past. Recognizing that discomfort occurs from emotions held from a past action, gave me the increased ability to reframe thoughts and possibly act more clearly and harmlessly in the future.

3. Energy Returning

While pondering the importance of being more in touch with something happening in daily life, I chance upon a newspaper article containing a picture of a friend from university days who is presenting a workshop. Taking a risk, I phone and we arrange to meet for lunch.

It turns out that his wife left him two years ago at approximately the same time as my husband. We are both in a lot of pain and we share a belief that a marriage is supposed to last a lifetime. He has brought a selection of family pictures. I sit quietly listening to his story, but he keeps asking questions regarding my husband, the last person I feel comfortable talking about.

Driving home, I feel invigorated and have a heightened awareness of all that's happening around me. This stimulation continues for several days and I take advantage of this new strength to finish a number of physically heavy outside tasks. Missing my friends and acquaintances from the twenty-one years we lived in Ontario, I am excited with the idea of perhaps having conversations over a coffee or lunch with a long-time friend. An enjoyment of life fills previous emptiness.

Beginning a fifth painting, size 24" x 24", I create a dominant black square box outline. Through the box opening, a tail escapes from a small solid black square inside.

Why is there this square with its stroke of paint oozing out the hole? Black is not a colour I like.

Fig. 5 Boxed

The colours inside the box and at the top of the painting are pink and gold.

I connect pink to feelings of love or kindness and yellow can mean light, happiness, and intellectual clarity. I call this painting, *Boxed.* (Figure 5)

Usually a period of time must pass before I fully understand my own message of colours and shapes. At the top of this painting I see that the pink and golden colours are much more obvious, less enclosed and freer. I conclude this perhaps represents my friend who obviously allows himself more space and freedom in expressing his feelings. I am afraid to express mine and enclose them in a sheltered, protected place.

Is it a fear of being vulnerable to possible rejection? I discern how boxed in I am. Apparently, I need the security of a safety zone. It's too frightening just now to be unguarded with another person. I don't feel I can trust anyone to be close to me.

Again, I take, what is for me, a huge risk. I phone this friend, a psychologist, and tell him I'm feeling vulnerable since our meeting. While talking together, I am totally shocked to find out he thought I didn't like him. It is then I understand the small black square emerging from the large protective square represents my fear. It is not knowingly masked, but it leaks out, becoming a repelling mechanism. How often do any one of us experience this from another person? Just bringing myself to admit my feeling has released some of the pent-up energy.

During childhood, when I came into the house, exuberant from my school day's events, my mother told me to go back outside and return quietly. During my marriage, I restrained my feelings because when I expressed them, I was belittled and accused of being too emotional. I have learned these lessons well, but today I find there's joy in acknowledging clearly what I feel.

Over the next few days, I complete four additional 24" x 24" abstract paintings. The colours I use now are clear bright red, gold and green. Lively energy flows into and through my brush. The colour and movement in the paintings tell me of returning vitality and I interpret these pictures as best I can. (Figures 6, 7, 8, and 9.)

I enjoy using the new colours and spontaneously creating with no planning of design. Nothing of emotional depth is occurring, but I appreciate a new aliveness and sense of adventure developing.

I've reached a plateau and nothing of a great significance or depth is surfacing. My psychologist now suggests I try a painting of my husband. He doesn't give me any other suggestions or directions as to imagery.

Fig. 6

Fig. 7

Fig. 8

Fig. 9

Boxed (Figure 5) and events surrounding this picture showed how I had protected my emotions. Remaining isolated and invulnerable in my comfort zone, I achieved a sense of security that was a self-imposed prison. I saw that feelings could leak out and emerge distorted. This could lead to misunderstanding between individuals and between groups. Partially and honestly expressing myself contributed to inner and enabling relief.

The set of four abstract paintings expressed newfound joy and happiness. Creating and moving to the present moment give me vitality, responsiveness, momentum and freedom. Although, I knew I needed to be careful how, and with whom I showed my vulnerability, I learned that mistakes could be acknowledged as stepping-stones. By taking a risk I was able to be freer from fear and live more fully.

4. Generations

As has been suggested by my therapist, it is now time to delve more deeply into my failed relationship. I'm unhappy about the idea of painting my husband and question the need to do this. Emotionally, or even technically, am I able to complete this project? Previously, I composed sketches and abstract free-style newsprint renditions showing both pleasant and unpleasant memories of our relationship. I now feel impelled to create a realistic picture, thus making the process much more formidable.

Looking for ideas I search through family records. Tears and grief seem bottomless. Finally, I find a snapshot of my husband taken about ten years earlier that includes one of my paintings given to him for his office. He stands gazing directly at the camera while holding his eyeglasses. I settle on this as the basis, and I want the figure to be life-size.

I am reading Alice Miller's book, *The Drama of the Gifted Child*, and am absorbed in understanding about damage done to all children, physically and emotionally. This includes destructive thoughts and actions retained by parents and grandparents from their childhoods. In addition to favourable modeling, these older inner child patterns are created and manifested in the following generation of children as the sins of the father/mother are passed along. The idea of transference along generational lines is very present in my consciousness. As I continue looking through old pictures, I discover a photo of my husband's grandfather and his adult children and decide this can illustrate the idea of previous generations.

I had met my husband while we were working in the Rockies during the summer of 1950. I wanted to be an artist, but at the end of high school my mother dissuaded me. She had women friends who took menial jobs during the Depression because they didn't have academic training and she was afraid, as an artist, that might happen to me. Educated women were expected to fill certain roles such as the traditional careers of teaching or nursing. I decided to attend university for a Home Economics degree and whenever possible, took as many art related courses as possible. At that time, approximately only five percent of the population continued on to post-secondary school. My husband and I were the first in our two families to graduate from a university.

In 1954 we married and I continued teaching in Vancouver as he completed his university degree. Shortly afterward, we moved to Alberta where our two daughters were born. Due to a job transfer, we moved to Victoria, BC where dissatisfaction led to my husband entering a doctoral program in Boston. Upon completion he accepted a teaching position in Ontario. By this time our eldest daughter was nine and had already attended four different schooling systems, in four cities and two countries.

In these years society still expected a woman to be a support for her husband and to look after children. A man was expected to be the provider and authority figure. We accomplished this pattern. I remained at home looking after our daughters. This decision was partly due to what I perceived as a need for our daughters to have something constant in their environment. I was also aware that because his mother had died when he was so very young, he wanted his children's mother to be home for them. As a child he had missed having her there and had needed his mother's love and support.

Working as a homemaker gave me the advantage of time and opportunity to develop my artistic abilities. During the 60s and into the early 80s, while living in Ontario, my participation in art classes and related activities increased. I studied art history at university and enrolled, as one of six members, in an experimental adult art program in a well-respected school. Here I developed skills in silk screening, silk painting, etching, weaving, life drawing, sculpture and painting. I enjoyed exhibiting in juried and group art shows, invitational exhibition and sales and finally my solo show. After creating a studio in our basement in one half of a converted double car garage, I could be found spending twelve to sixteen hours a day, happily working on art projects where, once I began, time just flew by. This was my natural milieu, an escape into joy.

To demonstrate that a child's life-setting patterns are formed at a very young age, I search for early pictures of our daughters. More remembrances of our lives together surface and my body aches.

Selecting a 30" x 40" canvas, I haltingly brush umber (brown) figures onto the canvas. My desire is to create the impression of the weight of the past expectations or beliefs draping over following generations. It's like words in a children's game I faintly recall from my childhood in which there was a saying, "Heavy, heavy hangs over thy head."

As this roughly painted sketch slowly emerges, unexpected nuances develop. Colouring my husband's tie, I instinctively use yellow instead of red and blue as shown in the photo. I add a yellow oval at the right side of the painting, I assume this was done to balance the yellow of the tie and the gold colour around my husband's inner child.

Fig. 10 Generations

Unexpectedly, haphazard brush strokes in the under layers of paint now display a face similar to the grandfather's and it appears in the body of one of his daughters! Is this a subconscious awareness surfacing in reference to patterns moving into younger generations?

Looking at the picture, I feel uneasy and decide to use white paint to cover my husband's piercing eyes. I'm happier with this eerie effect than when the eyes challenged the viewer.

Many memories materialize. My emotions surface strongly and to the point of nausea. It takes about a month of on and off painting to develop this rough interpretation. I can't complete it just now. As time passes I'll know if I want to do any more work on it.

For now, I call it *Generations.* (Figure 10)

Stuck again and still depressed, another challenge is presented by my psychologist. It is a strong recommendation that I paint my husband and me together. Again, I receive no directions as to style, size or content.

5. Marriage Breakdown

Reflecting on illustrating the two of us together, I decide to explore the theme of co-dependency. This idea seems appropriate, relatively safe and is currently prevalent in society. Trying to achieve some clarity, I spend ten days sorting through thirty years of family slides. It feels somewhat like being an unknowing lamb on its way to the slaughter and unaware of what lies ahead.

I start. I stop. I cry. I begin again and grieve some more. Memories, circulating thoughts, and regrets overwhelm me. I scream. I'm submerged in reliving the past. My grief about the loss seems bottomless. Other people assure me this will stop and new life will begin although it's difficult for me to see this right now. Is it necessary to do this painting? But my body feels a pressure of something demanding to be explored in order to understand what has happened as totally as possible. And so, I continue.

Escaping this painful process, I fall asleep while sitting in a living room chair. Jolted awake, I see in my mind's eye an image of the side edge of a large black blade slicing downwards in front of my face. It's what I imagine the guillotine might look and feel like.

Entering my art studio, I choose a white primed 24" x 30" canvas. Using black paint I quickly create a narrow, triangular shape giving the impression of the blade falling, cutting sharply through the emotional fields and ties between my husband and myself. An abstract rendition, rather than a picture of the two of us, feels safer to me just now.

Fig. 11 Anguish

Added streams of rainbow colours depict our energy fields. In front of my body, I sense a large gaping hole stretching from my neck to the top of my legs, as though energy has been pulled from me. It's trailing out and still attached to the departing energy of my husband. This action becomes subconsciously illustrated in the picture.

Centering myself, I experience a very strong contact with my inner anger. My brush, now filled with a clear, bright red, moves forcefully from the section of the painting that represents me, towards the solid black shape symbolizing the wall between us.

Contacting the hard blocking energy of that barrier, the red paint just drips and pours down the canvas as my grief pours out. The only name for this painting is *Anguish.* (Figure 11)

Eventually I return to the idea of picturing us together and gather illustrations to use as a guide in developing this theme. I choose our wedding photo. My second choice is a snapshot of us sitting in a small boat on a river in the Far East. I wear sunglasses and sit behind my husband. Weeding through family records of our family Christmas gatherings, I analyze the tilts of heads and body positions in groupings. I pencil small sketches illustrating our relationships to one another. This collection of information represents phases of our marriage, our family, and lastly just the two of us.

After organizing the placement of the three groups, I feel nauseous. It's a struggle facing these memories and so I leave the painting for a day or two.

Frustration sets in when I return to work on a 30" x 30" canvas and am unable to achieve the facial likenesses of my husband and myself. Perhaps a smaller brush might help? I resolve to purchase one the next time I'm near an art supply store. Interestingly though, I create good resemblances in the girls' faces. Stepping back from the picture after repainting my husband's face several times, I am surprised to see my father's likeness there. I rework that image. At the end of the day, I rest the painting against a wall to obtain a better view of the results and am startled to see that the faces have changed again and my husband's face now looks like my father's father! And the face, that was supposedly mine, is now a person unknown to me. Perhaps it is my husband's mother or grandmother? Are these alterations caused by rusty painting technique? Could some hidden knowledge be possibly appearing?

The next day I begin again and use white paint to cover my husband's eyes. After colouring in my sunglasses, earlier brush strokes form what appears to be an eye. In retrospect, was I unwilling to remove the sunglasses shading my vision on our situation or was it a form of self-protection while wishing the situation would either change or go away? My large white head signifies the degree of pain I'm feeling from the split relationship. Without giving it much thought, I give my husband a similar white head. Both heads have mouths wide open in silent screams. Single lines create the eyes. My head instinctively tilts upwards toward the family grouping, whereas my husband's head is offset on his neck but facing forward and to the side. This is not a conscious placement. They just seem to be accurately situated. These two abstract heads could be archetypes representing the distress generally present when partners go separate ways.

I am, at some inner level, aware that he too is feeling pain.

This undercoat layer that I have completed appears dull and missing accents. Therefore, in the wedding group, I place red in my husband's tie and the floral bouquet. (I can't recall these flowers. It's so long ago. Were there red roses? I'm not certain. I know that I wanted blue flowers and remember I couldn't find any.) Between the two of us, a splash of red represents a beginning split. Emphatically, and as a rupture between the white heads, I brush on red and brown paint.

Fig. 12 Breakdown

This picture is not about co-dependency, the theme I originally thought I was going to paint, but illustrates various stages of our marriage and the pain of separation. As a name, I first choose *Breakup* but settle on *Breakdown*. I don't know why, but this seems to be the best title. (Figure 12)

I have hit another plateau. Sometimes, I feel numbness, and every so often, there's just a steady pain. As I am stuck, a painting of myself is suggested for the next project.

Anguish dealt with my heartbreak. A vision gave me a direction to pursue and, in accepting it, I was able to address and to clarify my depth of pain. Having attachments to a person, belief, or situation created increased hurt when these were lost. To rediscover joy meant courageously walking through and exploring my emotional depths.

As the years passed, my husband and I shared experiences and psychic threads that bound us together. These were cut abruptly by the sudden departure. This rupturing of these connections is shown in the painting.

6. Breaking Out

Preparing to paint myself is more difficult. I have no one else with whom to compare; no other one to analyze, judge, or blame. I have nowhere to hide my own feelings and personal history. I face myself directly and this is scary.

Searching through family albums in my father's apartment, I discover very few photos of me from when I was a baby until six years old. My early years coincided with the early years of the Depression and there wasn't extra money for any luxuries. This is interesting because I also lack memories of almost all events in those years.

At the time my father is ninety years old and legally blind. He is a dignified and proud man who loves the water and ships and lives in a waterfront condo in Vancouver, BC. He was Worshipful Master of two Masonic Lodges, one of which he founded.

Living by himself, he values his independence. A special machine enlarges printing, helping him to read so that he is able to look after his financial affairs and records. It's stressful but it gives him something useful to do and keeps his mind active.

He traveled a lot and greatly misses being able to learn more about other places and people by reading newspapers or a good book. Even television is sometimes difficult for him to watch. He is tired of hearing the same old, still unresolved, world problems and often won't watch the news, preferring instead programs such as National Geographic.

Every few weeks I take this trip of four to six hours by car and ferry to visit him. We often go out for dinner, the meal he least enjoys preparing at home. While there, I complete errands for us both and this rushing around makes a stressful day or two for me.

While planning this painting of myself, I decide to make a visit. This time when I offer to help with things, he finds difficult to do; he illustrates his self-reliant spirit and refuses any aid. As he is restless and unhappy in the apartment, I suggest that we take a short drive to have dinner at one of his favourite restaurants. He insists he's too busy, an excuse he also gives to others when they invite him out.

Unable to treat him to an outing, I feel frustrated, disappointed and hurt. In spite of our deep connection to one another, neither of us is adept at expressing our feelings clearly and as a result, I leave to return home. I want to give him a change from his routine, but I also must respect his desire to live his life as he chooses.

As I get into the car to leave, my stomach is in knots and body tension is building. Not wanting this sense to accumulate, I drive away with car windows closed, and scream. My stomach eases somewhat. During the first months after my husband left, I did this frequently. Although I think screaming unpleasantly affects my body, I can think of no other way at this moment to release the pressure. Perhaps stopping for tea or a walk would be relaxing, but I fear that I would burst into uncontrollable tears.

In retrospect, we were both unhappy at this turn of events. I sadly wonder now why I didn't remain with him, letting go of my agenda, and patiently discover his?

After arriving home, the design of my self-portrait remains undetermined. Looking through teen-age photo albums, I find a snapshot of me sitting, hands folded in my lap, beside my high school boyfriend as we wait for a tennis court. My teen years were a happy, social and active time in my life so I decide to use this photo to represent my younger self.

In many pictures through the years, I sit quietly, in this same position. Admonitions, such as acting like a lady, dressing properly and appropriately for the occasion, and wearing matching colours of shoes, purse and gloves still rattle around, inhibiting me. I sometimes still feel anxious at seemingly not having, or not knowing, what is the best outfit to wear for an upcoming occasion and think perhaps I'd rather not go. It's well past time for me, as a well-known poem says, to wear purple and to walk barefoot in the grass regardless of what others think. Upon reflection, the choice of colour is not as important as feeling the freedom to just be myself.

The idea for a painting begins to form. The sections of my life I will bring together are myself as a young girl with my hidden inner child, my grandparents and parents, and a life size portrait of me at my present mature age. For this painting I choose a 30" x 30" canvas.

Beginning the undercoating, I paint my teenage-self in the background, sitting quietly, hands folded in my lap. My head is cut off just at eye level. I'm not sure why I've placed myself in this position. What are my thoughts? I'm quite conscious of the watching elders peering over my shoulder. The chain, or connecting thread, reaches from the past generations around my teenager's inner child, then behind my adult neck and over my shoulder up to the throat of my head in the foreground. Is it what is stopping my voice?

Looking closely and intently in a mirror, I painstakingly paint teeth and tongue showing in my open mouth. I am naked and hold the steering wheel of a car firmly in both hands illustrating control and determination. Is there also fear?

Fig. 13 Breaking Out

My scream coming from my inner depths appears stuck and buried deep inside. Is there only one scream, or more? I will continue the painting after finding a way to release my voice. The title will be *Breaking Out.* (Figure 13)

I speak quietly and, earlier, my students learned to be attentive while receiving working instructions. I wonder if singing lessons might loosen my voice? I sang briefly in a university choir but in order to keep my notes in tune, I was sandwiched between two other singers. I always thought I couldn't carry a tune. Deciding to take some lessons, I am greatly surprised when the teacher informs me that my voice actually has true pitch and a two-octave soprano range!

For now, I leave this painting and my stuck scream and proceed with the suggestion of painting myself as a child.

7. The Child's Gift

When beginning this series of paintings, the original illustration coming to mind is one of me as a child. I know this is an important picture for me to do but my feelings, relationships, and passages of growth are safer to be explored before uncovering this younger person. It is usually necessary to work from the present to the past and so it is logical for me to work from my husband, the relationship, myself and finally, earlier years. The metaphor of peeling an onion is a good example. Outer skins of thin layers slip off very easily. The next, more compact layers are pulled off in pieces and sections. The solid inner core, the beginning, is the last to appear and the innate child is slowly revealed layer by layer. Now I am ready to try to understand this early part of me. This painting will be life size on a 36" x 48" canvas. I feel intimidated, as it's been a long time since I have attempted anything this size. There's also my fear of dropping the mask and revealing a part of me that seems very tender and more precious than shown in any rendition of a mature human being.

The special photo chosen is one taken just a few months past my third birthday. Here I stand on a stone garden path in front of our house and hold a golden chrysanthemum. Using tones of umber, a full sketch rapidly emerges. A heavy feeling develops between my heart and throat and I leave the picture and sleep for a couple hours. When I awaken, a feeling of aloneness fills me. As an only child I often felt this way and I use this word carefully, differentiating from loneliness. Again, in the evening I fall asleep while sitting in a chair. This process is requiring a lot of energy. Drawing a child's proportions is a new art experience for me and I struggle with this aspect. Proceeding slowly, I roughly brush in the facial features and finally feel satisfied that the emotions displayed in the painting. My lack of trust is clear.

Several times over the next two days, I redo the floor, legs and feet. No matter how hard I try, this child does not stand firmly. I cannot ground her, so decide to allow her to float. Usually my painting skill is able to solve this problem, but not this time. It possibly shows that I myself am not yet grounded and I believe this may be affecting the painting. For now, the painting is simply called *A Young Child.* (Figure 14)

Fig. 14 Young Child

It's time for a break in this process. My creativity and willingness to explore further is hesitant.

Years later, after reading this chapter and showing a snapshot of the early, *A Young Child,* to my writers' group, a member wondered aloud why the hands were so large and the legs so small. I passed this off as simply a difficulty in rendering proportions. Quickly though, I realized that my hands were my artist's tools and a very important part of me. Apart from some drawing ineptitude, my legs could perhaps refer to a physical weakness. As I grew, my leg bones strengthened and lengthened but the muscles didn't keep pace. As a result, occasionally when walking home from elementary school, my knees buckled and I landed on them on the concrete sidewalk. I've never been a strong walker. Perhaps, looking at my age three picture, there was a subconscious recognition of these physical characteristics.

8. Floor Mat

Something restrains my creativity flow and I desire a change in direction. Therefore, I decide to attend a two-day workshop on how to produce a painted floor mat and hopefully develop a new inspiration. These cotton canvas mats painted with acrylic paints are then varnished and placed at doorways, under dining room furniture, or wherever else you would like a rug. They protect the floor, are decorative and easily cleaned.

I arrive with great intentions to create a mat harmonizing with a fireplace brick wall visible as one enters the front entrance to my home. A group of nine women are present and we begin the morning by practicing techniques on 12" x 18" canvases. I want to forgo this amount of training, and I get three small works done by lunchtime. They are not very inspiring and I am quite disinterested in them. I really want to get on with *my project.*

Afternoon arrives and I can now begin creating my brick wall. As I add colours the matt-to-be is covered with realistic life size bricks joined with grouting. I enjoy working the varying desert-rock colours. Then I add shadows and wiggly lines to indicate both the substance and cracks inherent in bricks. Finally, placing the canvas on the floor, I stand and regard with dismay a solid, forbidding brick wall lying on the floor. A friend passes by and tells me to at least hang a frying pan on the bricks. All I can think of illustrating here is a spider eating a squashed fly. Am I that squashed fly? She then suggests I could perhaps create some holes in the wall. I wonder if these could include outdoor scenes. It's the end of the day and nothing is resolved. Tomorrow is another day and hopefully new ideas will appear.

Returning the next morning and having no additional inspiration, I spend time repainting the bricks. In the afternoon, to illustrate bits of sparkle, I add an iridescent glaze all over. After barging ahead with this now, not so brilliant idea, I sadly realize that the life of the bricks has disappeared, just as I shield myself. I am unhappy and discouraged at the prospect of repainting.

Upon reflection, I remember my grandmother's words of "More haste, less speed," and of my mother telling me that no one knows how much time I spend on a project, they only see the result. Now I confront a life pattern of rushing ahead enthusiastically and then regretting the outcome, wishing that I had worked it out in a different way. Perhaps some discipline and slower, smaller steps will reduce overwhelming feelings regarding new changes and directions.

I regard my day as unsuccessful, a waste of energy and having little creativity. I am frustrated and judge myself for not being able to access the part of me that is stuck. This attitude is neither helping me inwardly nor easing the current situation.

Workshops are never my best atmosphere for creating. When I paint, I prefer to be away from other people and quietly connect with whatever I sense that is happening in the work. I know that I always create best in a space of silence.

The weekend is over and I pack up my supplies, roll up my *wall* and assume I will complete it at home, little realizing that a new event is going to propel me forward.

9. Meeting Again

While driving to meet my husband, my heart feels full of a mix of apprehension, hope, love and also anger of how he could do this to us. There is still a dream inside me that we may again be together with an improved relationship. My intent is to try to heal our wounds, not by a lot of talking, but by being present in this moment and possibly make a reconnection with the person I had lived with for so many years.

We eat a well-prepared and tasteful dinner. The conversation centers on generalities and safe topics such as what the children are doing. There is certainly no discussion of meaningful issues between us. Nor can I express any of my anger at the manner of his parting. I am still afraid of self-assertion and the possible resulting confrontation.

After dinner, we part with tears in our eyes and a hug. He is on his way to Sweden for business and staying with a mutual woman friend. I am returning to my island. This old pattern of him leaving on business trips while I remain at home triggers other memories of former times.

Once in the car, I fall to pieces with tears, choking and giving the occasional scream. I focus intently on the car, the road and my driving. It is a quiet time to drive and I thankfully arrive, twenty-three miles later, safely at the ferry terminal. I feel so vulnerable.

I now feel compelled to complete the large personal paintings begun in that period that seems a long time ago.

The next day I grab a 24" x 36" canvas and immediately begin brushing on the golden colour of California poppies. At the moment these are my favourite flowers. They are survivors, strong and yet bending in the wind. Their lively colours are full of life and energy. I know that my choice of flowers can be a reflection of how I see my real self, or how I would like to be seen.

Cautiously, I create vague forms of gently swirling brilliant golden-orange with the dark blue of space itself in the background. Symbolically I am painting my husband and myself, but why do I also place a third poppy between us in the background? I assume this is done to balance the colours and shapes.

In the next meeting with my psychologist, I tell him of my experience and the meaning of the painting. He also questions why is there a third flower? I have no answer.

During the following days, details slowly emerge. The flaming colours contrast greatly against the background of varied dark blues and greens and purples blending together. Vibrancy of life fills the painting. Elements, sketchily added, have a quality of freshness.

In a couple of weeks, I receive a surprise phone call from my husband. He says he doesn't want me to hear the news from someone else, but events have changed. The woman in Sweden has now become very important to him. My guess is that he was also feeling vulnerable after our meeting and, perhaps, if some other person was in my life at this time, I would have a similar story to relate. But I don't.

A day or so later, I return to the almost completed painting. A lightning thought occurs. Could it be possible that my subconscious already knew of the new situation and this is the reason the third poppy is here? Too many other unexpected happenings have appeared throughout my whole painting process for this idea to be declared impossible.

Fig. 15 Meeting Again

It then becomes somewhat humorous deciding which poppy is which person! I really like this painting and call it *Meeting Again*. I do not think I will hang it on my wall. (Figure 15)

Considering his new relationship and its effect on me, I feel compelled to complete the large personal paintings begun in a period that seems a long time ago, although it's only been a few years.

10. Observing Patterns

One day I listened to tapes of Deepak Chopra discussing the DNA molecule containing our genealogical information that is in each of our cells. This holograph of an individual's evolution appears as our personal design. Thus, every one of us has an internal key to understand how we have become as we are. My search included looking over generational patterns of thoughts and actions and to find out how these affected my outlook on life.

My mother's parents emigrated from a village in Wales near Swansea to Cumberland, BC where she was born in 1904. They later moved to Vancouver, BC where she grew up with her older brother and three sisters, two older and one younger. They were not allowed to dance, play cards, drink or smoke. They walked twice to a Baptist church on Sundays. Her mother was like a mother hen with her brood and, through the years, organized many extended family dinners.

Mother was the one individual who broke free of many of her family restrictions. She became an elementary school teacher, relinquishing this at marriage. She sewed most clothes for me, including tailoring a wool Black Watch plaid suit. Her bridge club members continued as close friends for many years. When I was in my late teens, she began a pottery avocation, exhibiting locally and in juried traveling shows from which the National Art Gallery purchased one piece.

Mother, her mother and myself assumed caretaker roles. Many common every day machines of today hadn't been invented and we spent time doing what is now called slow cooking, preserving fruits and even preserving eggs in brine. Iceboxes with weekly delivery of blocks of ice kept food cool. Hard wax applied to floors and rubbed to a shine by hand continued until a wonderful machine was invented having brushes to spread the wax, the brushes then covered with sheep wool pads completed the buffing. Clothes, washed and put through wringers to remove most of the water, were hung outside on lines to dry. In freezing weather, they froze stiff. Time wasn't available to expand one's horizons to fully develop individual potential, capabilities and dreams.

I never particularly cared for my mother's father. To explore this feeling, I tried holotropic breath work under my psychologist's guidance. This involved lying down, listening to music, eyes closed, breathing very deeply and rapidly until I relaxed into an expansive inner space. The first two sessions I traveled inwardly to sensing and seeing some images of past cultural eras. But, when I completed the third session, and surprising us both, my right-hand palm firmly covered my right ear and my mouth opened wide in a silent scream. For approximately ten minutes I was unable either to remove my hand or to close my mouth, even though trying very hard to do both. I sensed a man's pudgy hand hitting me hard on the right side of my head. It was not my father's, as his hand had long slender fingers. It appeared to be mother's father's hand. Could this be true? It definitely appeared so from my experiences and recollection of that part of family life.

Throughout my life many right ear problems such as infections occurred, and a serious one put me in hospital at a young age, apparently delirious. Of course, this was long before penicillin or other pharmaceutical drugs. Years later during an airplane landing, this eardrum burst. My hearing in this ear had diminished over the years and so during my personal searching, I decided on an operation to replace this eardrum. During relaxing massages in the weeks before entering the hospital, images arrived in my mind's eye. Unexpectedly as my head and neck were massaged, the first image was my grandfather's moustache and in the second, his whole face appeared. This seemed to confirm my earlier assumption regarding the hit on my head. Absolutely no thoughts or emotional recollections were present, but my young child's memory was firmly encased only in my physical body. Obviously much unconscious information is not only in our emotional and mental fields but is submerged and unknown in us physically. How many previous generations send information flowing into our cells? What amount of our current body problems or illnesses does this explain?

My father, born in 1902 in a village near Leeds, England played freely in the fields surrounding his home. His father immigrated by himself to Canada while the children were young. Did he intend to send for his family? I think this was unlikely as in my Nana's journal, she wrote that she refused to be left alone in England to bring up three children who she felt were also her husband's responsibility.

And so she, a strong independent woman, emigrated bringing Dad and his younger sister and brother to Canada. Arriving in Vancouver, she was surprised to find her new home was only a tent on what was later the PNE (Pacific National Exhibition) grounds. Luckily someone took pity on this young family and found a room for them in a nearby barn.

When Nana moved to Canada she brought her sewing machine from England and continued sewing for her family and others. My Christmas presents were wonderful useful creations that were labeled "Bits 'n Batts" as they were made from miscellaneous fabric scraps. She also fixed up one residence after another. I recall her painting ceilings of rooms in her home while in her 80s. Later she wrote a journal, filling a soft covered notebook. I am sure that writing her story helped release much of her lifetime pain. It told why she married my grandfather, what her life was like and detailed her disappointment and anger about her marriage. She had realized shortly after marriage that her husband was still a child in many ways. As she also believed that children should be seen and not heard, perhaps this is why my daughters say they do not recall ever hearing my dad's father, Bapa, speak. Unfortunately, as boys grow, they hear about not showing their feelings. I think this restricts many men's emotional maturity.

I followed the routine of making drapes, painting walls and generally increasing the quality of each of our residences where our average time of stay was approximately two-and- one half years. I sewed clothing and many gifts for my family. And here I am in my seventies, also writing a story about my life and marriage.

I resemble Nana in many ways. I laugh like her and have her strong will. Frustrating my father, I cleared things out on impulse just like she and Dad's sister did. I married not only because that was expected of a woman in my generation but also like her, I gained independence from my family situation. Bapa, Dad's father, built a variety of homes and in this process of constant moving my father went to twelve different schools before university. Bapa was an impractical dreamer. He was also very creative and in the late 1920s, according to a family tale, designed a blade to wipe rain from car windows: a novel idea. Someone else patented the invention. I have felt close to this grandfather-of-few-words who began painting in his late eighties. Never having had an art lesson in his life, his second picture was a landscape with natural perspective both in relative size and colour relationships. Unfortunately, he completed only a few works before turning blind a couple of years later. He had much undeveloped, unrecognized creativity (by himself as well as others). That artistic talent in him is also in me.

Nana became blind in her nineties and yet, while in a nursing home, at 100 years old she was still able to sing the chorus from Handel's Messiah that she had sung as a young woman. Bapa died in his 90s.

Dad constantly built, remodeled or improved things around our home. He designed and built a pottery studio in our basement for my mother. His real desire had been to become an architect. At the end of his first year of university he was offered a summer job by Bapa who, when autumn arrived, didn't have enough money available for the following year fees. Dad didn't return to his studies and not reaching his desired goal was a lifetime disappointment.

He was also disappointed in his father, who was a poor provider and therefore a lot fell on his mother to fill family needs. This was usually done by her sewing and housekeeping. I also considered a career as an architect. I believe our residences contribute to molding our attitudes. I enjoy the challenge of conceptualizing and creating living areas. During marriage I designed a house, hiring a contractor to build it. The year before our marriage ended, I combined my talents with those of an architect to build another house on Salt Spring Island.

Was this dream mine or was I continuing Dad's unfinished ambition? I doubt my mathematical ability is strong enough to understand and develop mechanical stresses for building. My thinking process is circular and spatial, not linear. I think children often ignore their particular talents and take on a job of completing their parent's unfinished aspiration. This may happen more than we realize.

After my mother died, Dad eventually remarried. After my stepmother died, he lived by himself until hospitalized, just after turning ninety-three. Early one morning, five weeks after his birthday, he told a nurse it was time for him to leave. She didn't pay attention and so he told another. Unfortunately, no one phoned me and very sadly for us, about 10 a.m. that day, he passed on, independent as ever, and alone. I hope I can have that amount of will, acceptance and clarity when it's my time to leave.

I'm sure that with more time and desire I could have further continued tracing back family members. Was it important to do this exercise? I think so because I better understood my parent's actions, gaining compassion for them and also myself. Studying even a few individuals revealed various traits and characteristics affecting me and gave me knowledge that became my freedom to freely choose to change my life. Perhaps it will show others that they also have that option.

11. Generations: Continued

Soon after completing *Meeting Again*, I continue working on *Generations*. It has been a couple of years since I began this picture. First, I brush additional brown and grey tones over the background, and clarify the faces there. I redo the hands and fingers of the children. While looking at my husband's face, I experience sorrow when perceiving that I have painted it with love and caring.

I feel blocked again. Tears of frustration slide down my face and I want to run away from my pain and sadness. I realize there's nowhere to escape because these feelings are inside me, a part of me, and they go with me until I acknowledge them and become aware of the underlying cause.

Many years ago, when I had a deep physical ache in my neck and could tolerate it no longer, I lay down on the living room rug and relaxed into a new acceptance of the agony. Finally, I felt energy break through and out the back of my neck leaving me with feelings of joy and no pain. At that moment, I realized that by not resisting but by taking the action of walking through a situation, I could bring myself to a place of ease. Therefore, it is logical to me that when the cause of my current unhappiness is uncovered, I will achieve some peace. For the moment, though, I leave the painting.

Days pass before I return to add blue on the clothes, then a deep, dark blue under the children and around my husband's hand. Details are augmented on the children's faces and their clothing. I paint a wedding ring on my husband's finger. That does it. Immediately, tears fall and I quit for the day.

The following day, I paint a shape under the children to represent a magic flying carpet and another wave effect along the bottom of the picture to illustrate movement in life. Added paint emphasizes the eyeglasses held in the hand. When I place additional colour to the wedding ring. I decide *Generations* is complete. (Figure 16)

A few days later I show this painting to my therapist. Noting the white child under my husband's arm, he questions if I instinctively painted it that way. Does it indicate a scarcity in my husband's life as a child? I don't know if that was the reason, but it is a logical thought because there was a lack of both money and emotional support in his childhood. Not only did his mother, through death, leave this young child, but also his older siblings had helped to raise him, while they were involved with their own growing up. His father seldom showed emotions or gave praise.

As I discuss my reactions to the wedding ring, I am asked what I want to say to my husband. It is very difficult to start but once begun, my words stream forth and I am surprised at the many repressed feelings. Memories flooding my mind and heart are spoken. The flow of feelings seems unending and travels in many directions. It also indicates my strong belief about the wedding ring symbolizing of the permanence of wedding vows.

After releasing these past memories and feelings, I suddenly become acutely aware of the impermanence of everything in my life. The only relevant time or action is a particular moment and one second later it becomes the past. My previous future is now my present time. It reminds me of watching the patience and beauty of monks kneeling and building a mandala (a metaphor for life) with minute grains of sand. Various colours (or experiences) create the mandala.

Fig. 16 Generations Completed

After it's completed and has sat for a while, the time arrives for everything to end (or transition). The grains are gathered up and returned to the ocean in order to illustrate the transient quality of our lives. And the process begins again. I deeply experience the sense of the transitory essence of life and its constant change.

Much of life is about movement. Without recognizing this quality and maintaining it actively in my life, I stagnate. In stagnation, there is a presupposition of death. Moving on to new events and stages of my life creates action and so, perhaps now I can finally accept that a wedding ring often reflects only an illusion.

Generations covered many ideas concerning our modern family. At a later time, I wondered if I subconsciously painted the tie yellow, the same colour as the *yolk* surrounding my husband's inner child, because a tie, as a symbol, shows how a person can be choked, just as one is suffocated emotionally by an unacknowledging inner child. Perhaps the covered eyes, removing the penetrated stare, signified either an unwillingness or inability to accept the idea of hidden feelings, or the manner in which past events and actions affect our current relationships.

This picture of my husband, our children, and his ancestors led me to understand more clearly the veiled influences of ancestors. When what appeared to be the face of my husband's grandfather showed in a yellow oval on the image of his daughter, the idea of the stream of consciousness passing through generations was visually presented. Even as a trained artist, creative energy developed unexpected nuances as in facial changes. Symbolic changes of colour occurred and what could have been assumed to be an accident was, in fact, some kind of inner wisdom manifesting. None of these paintings in my process were planned ahead in any detail.

Most of us turn a blind eye to the controlling influences within and around us. Because of all the regulations during my childhood, I was aware of, and even felt, the weight of previous generations' thoughts and pressures affecting my consciousness and actions. These ancient streams not only affect me, but my current family, the people in my neighbourhood and town, and in our countries.

We are all influenced by the past as well as by individual role models in our childhood. We copy good and poor behavior of our elders and these actions are perpetuated by passing them on to our children and then to their children.

Our resistance to change may be caused by fears, inertia, or a variety of desires and greed. However, it is my impression that beliefs can cause the greatest obstruction. Supporting and encouraging words, even one genuine word of acknowledgement to someone in despair, can influence successful change in a life path. Hopefully, respect and non-violent words and actions will eventually become the human norm.

Does a strong judgment regarding right and wrong lead to separateness and to isolation of individuals and groups? Does it lessen compassion? I think that strong beliefs may cause the greatest obstruction toward being receptive to alternate solutions and wonderful possibilities. Clear thinking and goodwill are required to courageously stand against peer pressure in order to innovate and/or consider the good of others, rather than only oneself or selected groups and individuals. I decided it was in my power to change the direction of thought patterns and actions inherited in my family. We all have this creative power and we can use it for our personal future and also for the common good.

12. Marriage Breakdown: Continued

It had been nearly two years since I've worked on this painting illustrating the sequence of events from our marriage ceremony to having a family, facing the pain in the partnership, and finally the eventual breakup.

In earlier paintings I used rainbows and their reflections to illustrate the changing quality of life. Here, the gold, painted around the marriage ceremony symbolizes joy present in this event and the green surrounding the family represents growth of the family unit.

Perhaps the blue added around our heads is for growing uneasiness.

Eventually, I add clothing to the family group so they do not stand in isolation as non-relating heads. Our family members have quite separate abilities and each works at developing these attributes. Although we did many things together, there was always present this quality of individuality rather than dependency. (Figure 17)

Satisfied with the painting, I show it to my art therapist. While sitting in his office and looking at the picture, a strong feeling wells up inside me. My husband's head is dominant in each area. His head is in the center of the painting and is the focal point here, just as he was in my life. A rejecting response erupts. Unhappily I regard my work in reaction to the authoritative quality showing in the relationship. Accepting that I allowed the situation to develop I must now face the reality of my feelings.

Fig. 17 Marriage Breakdown

Fig. 18 Marriage Breakdown: Separateness

I am asked what I am going to do about my dilemma. I find I have several choices. I can remove my husband's face, or I can remove my own head, thereby taking me out of the situation. My third option is to leave the painting as it is and not destroy a completed canvas. It is not an option to allow it to remain as it is. My nausea increases as I continue looking at the painting.

Finally, grasping scissors, I cut and tear my head out from the painting. Symbolically: I am free but I am also alone.

Still unhappy with my husband's head I grab up various coloured felt markers to cover his face. This affects a change in the feeling of power structure. No longer is this completed canvas regarded as precious or lasting. This compares with my marriage. In addition, with my separated head placed to one side, I understand the beauty in my separateness. (Figure 18)

Returning home with two pieces of painted canvas, it's clear that the most important aspect for me is the process of creating, rather than the finished project. Also, whatever appears completed, either an object or my life situation, is not permanent and can be either destroyed or recreated. It's a freedom of choice as long as harmlessness prevails.

What can I do now with our faces? My inner art critic tells me the work with coloured markers is careless. I toy with the idea about cleaning off the colours. Another thought is to cut out my husband's head and glue it onto the upper left side of the painting, perhaps adding an antique frame around it. My face placed onto a separate canvas could develop into a new painting. I don't settle on any of these options. I need a break from this work.

A couple of weeks later I receive a call from my husband. Almost immediately after hanging up the phone, my old reaction of powerlessness slides into place. Marching into the studio, I pick up scissors and take his crayoned head right out of the canvas creating two holes. Now we are both removed from this scene and there are two holes. Rolling my husband's head, I tie it with a ribbon and glue it beside the marriage group. It looks like a diploma in the memory section. Taking action instead of sitting helplessly in reaction to the phone call invigorates me.

Choosing a second canvas, I paint a blue sky over an area that will show through the holes in the first canvas. Then, cutting the original canvas painting carefully along the top of the lines shaping the two white heads, one half of each head is rolled down to create spaces where the blue on the second canvas behind. New activities can be illustrated here but at the moment I lack interest. This lack of vitality corresponds with my own uncertainty about how to fill the empty space in my life.

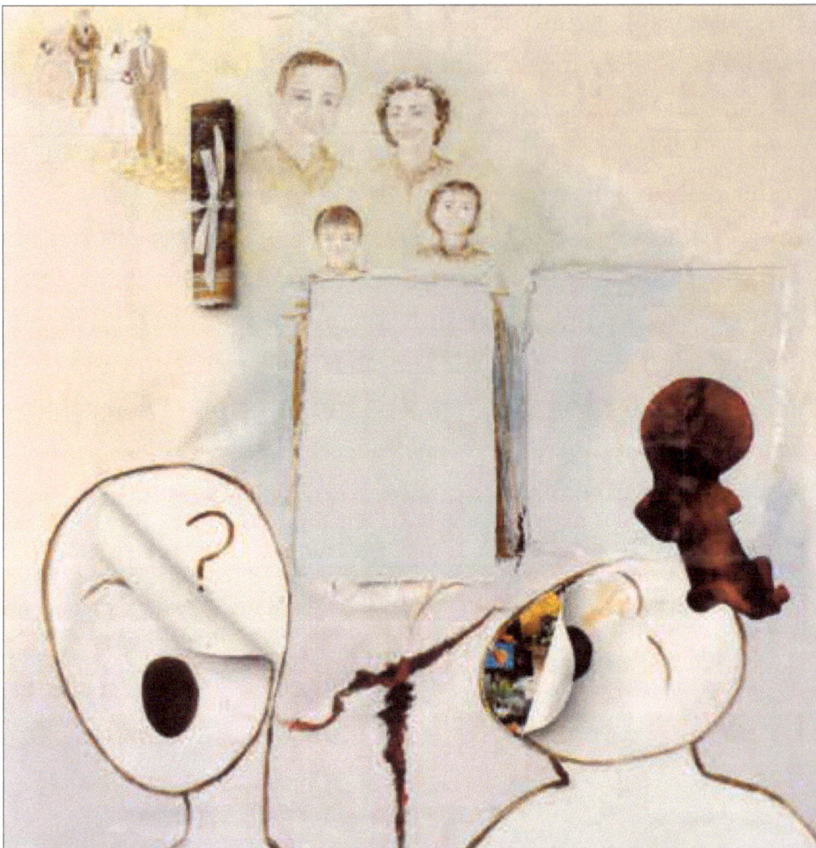

Fig. 19 Marriage Breakdown: New Life

The following week I remove the second blue canvas from its stretched frame, gluing it behind the first canvas to create blue sky in the holes. Now I need to decide on ideas for filling the areas behind the rolled heads.

Flipping through old snapshots for possible ideas, I cry while sorting through too many past memories. Stopping and changing direction, I find old magazines to cut pictures of positive activities, such as tennis, sailing, skiing, and hiking. These will be pasted under my head. Thinking the selection's not complete, I continue until I see a photograph of a fetus that feels exactly right. I'm not sure why this illustration absolutely fills my requirement, but I cut it out.

When placing the photograph on the canvas, I realize it's a little male. How can this represent anything of me in this painting?

I try different placements but he seems to be too large for me to hide his penis. Finally, I decide he represents the energy of my new strength being born. I place him in a blue-sky space. Golden rays show a tunnel of light bringing the baby to earth. I paint a question mark under my husband's rolled head, as I don't know what's going on there and paste some activity illustrations in the space under my head.

Humorously and reminiscent of the movie about the *Wizard of Oz*, I enjoy painting a yellow brick road in front of the wedding procession. There doesn't seem to be anything else I want to add just now. (Figure 19)

Showing this newly completed painting in my therapy session, a discussion ensues, during which I become aware that the masculine aspect of me is still young and growing. A question is asked about why the scroll of my husband's head is retained and is so well stuck onto the canvas? I am not sure but it seems that creating this scroll represents a passage of time and a work completed. I still have not yet released this past life completely. Several thoughts come to mind but perhaps I can release an attachment to some of the past and so I remove this scroll from the painting. This subject seems complete for now.

Several years later, increased meaning had developed regarding a variety of features. When I first painted the yellow brick road, I thought it humorous that I could look at the journey this way. Later, I realized it also signified the fantasy of a storybook marriage.

Marriage Breakdown illustrated a progressive detachment, and conveyed the value of analyzing a situation and communicating without fear as one travels along. Although I could see the potential of my partner's Soul, I forgot that it was for him to find and develop, and I actually lived with that personality. I think many women, and for many reasons, make the same mistake of looking at the possibility-rather than what is living in front of them.

Supporting my husband's needs, growth and career left little room for me to do the same for myself. At least sixteen years after I had worked outside the home, I was offered a university lecturer's position. My husband gave his verbal support, but I sensed a strong underlying current of resistance to me working outside the home. I eventually turned down the job. Returning home to find him sitting in the living room I told him the news. His response of, "Thank Goodness," shocked me. It validated my intuitive sensing cautioning me to pay attention to my gut instinct.

13. Breaking Out: Continued

The inner urge to complete these paintings continues and as I return to painting myself, I feel very alone. My scream is still not vocal in this picture; it buried deeply inside. With it hidden, I am safe with familiar and known situations, and my feelings are secure inside.

Irrationally, I shed tears and ask questions. Where's me? What are my needs, my hungers, and my passions? How can I express them? I feel imprisoned. And yet, this is an illusory protective boundary.

In the studio, I pick up *Breaking Out* and spread a coloured glaze onto the background. Shadows and highlights added to my body flesh enliven the image. The four faces of my grandparents are above me and the two faces of my parents peering beside me are defined more carefully. Strengthened lines on my teenager's clothing accidently form a cage around my inner child.

Gradually, to illustrate a scream, tentative brush strokes of red emerge from my mouth. I stop. Once these lines are done, they are there to stay. Additional colour might obliterate the detailed expression on my face. Then I notice that during repainting my body flesh, the chain trailing from my grandparents up to my throat has disappeared. Is this an indication that my scream is ready to be released? At this point, I again stop for a while.

Am I ready to release family beliefs? I wonder if I am frightened of ruining this painting or am I resisting that inner scream? Is it possible that with all the nausea I've had during this unearthing process, I may actually, as is mentioned in some shaman books, need to materially throw up this strangled cry?

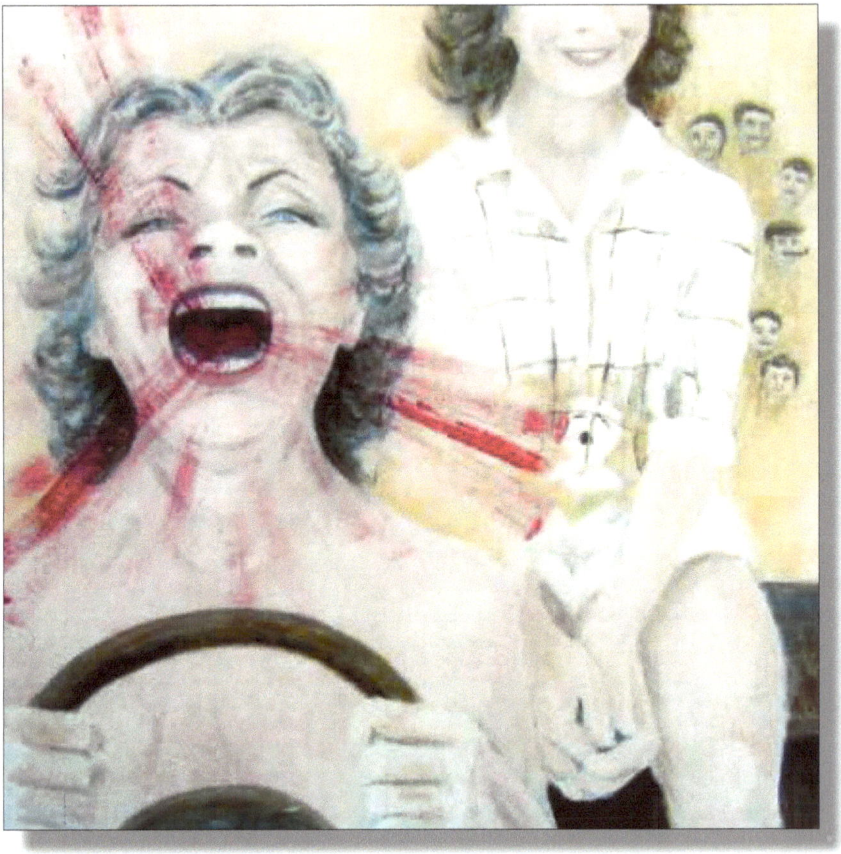

Fig. 20 Breaking Out Complete

Several days later, courage arrives to create additional red lines and thicken some of the first lines. I stop when the scream seems to be surfacing in the painting. Interestingly this process also begins to break the lines in the clothing around my repressed inner child. These lines are representing expectations by others that I live my life in prescribed ways.

It is a very slow process to peel away layers of conditioning residing in my subconscious. (Figure 20)

It is obvious the teenager, even though sitting so properly, is happier than the present adult. Perhaps, when I totally release stifled emotions, I will be able to break free and become the real person I am.

Breaking Out showed a happier younger person. My naked body symbolized the desire, as well as the necessity, to disregard all unnecessary programming from my parents and their parents ad infinitum. I needed to begin fresh to create my true individuality. My tight hold on the driving wheel illustrated determination and also the depth of my craving to find and know my course in life.

This pictured scream struggles to surface, to be released and enable me to speak my own truth. This could be compared to a baby taking its first breath, crying as it is pushed from the mother's womb and into the cold earth environment. An unfamiliar life begins with new adventures and ways of learning ahead. In this freedom, it is possible to take the best of all and to recreate my own particular journey.

14. Release

Reaching this nearly conclusion point in my process, I take three paintings to my therapist. These are: *Generations*, *Marriage Breakdown*, and *Breaking Out*. During a long session, we discuss the paintings in detail and explore some of the finer points of my developing awareness. I experience a strange relaxing of body tensions that continue later when I am at home.

Strong vibrations manifest in my jaw, across my clavicle, and along my arms and into my hands. Additional undulations ripple down my neck and into the top of my shoulder blades. An incredible degree of stress is dispersing. Pulsations in my back and arms slowly subside, but I still experience throbbing in my jaw and my hands for about six more hours. Then, I totally relax and sleep soundly.

Needing to create a ceremony to help complete our marriage and separation, I take the canvas *Marriage Breakdown* outside the next day, and use two sticks to prop it up. In front, I place the snapshot of my husband I used as a basis of *Generations*. Beside this I stand our wedding photo, as well as the small wooden sculpture he brought back from a trip. Finally, ceremoniously I light one match and burn it all. (*Releasing Marriage* - Figure 21)

During the burning, I feel instant relief. Afterwards though, tears and grieving flow. My security has been totally shaken by my husband's leaving. I do trust, though, that after walking through this painful period something new will be created.

Fig. 21 Releasing Marriage

A strong inner desire develops to burn the remainder of the paintings. This feeling increases, filling and pushing inside my chest. I busy myself with household chores. I drive and pick up groceries. Occupying my time with miscellaneous activities helps me resist this almost constant urge to put a match to my extensive painting efforts.

Very early the next morning I waken with a dream that continues as I become conscious. Many words and paragraphs about the paintings form in my mind. I am sure I will remember everything but then again, perhaps I won't so while half awake, I rapidly write the words onto paper. When finished, I reread and edit the pages. Because this is too early for my day to begin, I curl up in bed. About one-half hour later I give up on any idea of sleeping, sit up and read over the morning dream words, delete all the earlier editing and leave the prose as it was first written. Seeing these 500 words as an introduction to a book, I wonder if my process will ever end. I have no idea about writing a book! I still have a strong urge to start a fire.

After eating breakfast and watching some television, my unreasonable need to *do* something remains. This feeling is so persistent that I phone my psychologist and ask if he has any particular requirement for the paintings. As usual, he's very careful to allow me space and to have me to take responsibility for my decisions. Out of habit, I would much rather have a solution suggested or even be told what would be the best thing for me to do. He suggests that what I do is my decision and that this is *my* process. After the phone call, I struggle to ignore the idea of burning, but it is becoming a compulsion. What is it that I am really trying to expel?

Upon reflection, I remember that I have casual slides and snapshots of various stages of the process. On the other hand, I recall how the compositions exerted a powerful effect on individuals who have seen them. Therefore, my dilemma, about whether or not I should burn the paintings?

Finally, I act. Entering the studio area, I pick up a sharp knife and cut all the canvases from their stretcher frames except the one of me as a child and the one with the three golden poppies called *Meeting Again*. This results in a pile less than one half inch on the floor. An increased feeling of lightness and more space develops in the studio.

Rolling the pieces of canvas together, I take them outside and place the collection in the brick concrete burner in the backyard. To record this coming event, I set up two cameras: an automatic one for slides, and a friend holds the other camera for prints. Only one lighted match on a canvas causes months of work to transform into ashes in less than ten minutes. I am stunned at this speed. (*Releasing Generations* Figure 22; Figure 23)

My strongest feeling after this event is a sense of the finite quality of life itself. Obviously, each minute in time has its own special importance and, yet, it is also simply one single, fleeting instant. Life moves immediately forward to the next moment.

The following morning, I regret burning *Generations* and *Breaking Out*, two of my strongest paintings with regard to style and content. They will never be created again. Yet there was also much past personal life and pain in them.

Did I need to keep them longer? I don't know. Possibly there are other agendas for the paintings. The slides could be used for other classes, or for a lecture tour, or for a book. Perhaps, though I can consider doing things just as a means toward a goal. Simply being in each moment is all that's necessary.

By not holding on to precious thoughts or things in my impermanent existence, I create space for a new quality of life to emerge in each second. If I act directly from my heart, I will be fully alive. This is a challenge.

Fig. 22 Releasing Generations

Fig. 23 Releasing Generations

Fig. 24 Poppies

15. Poppies

I feel I have completed all I want to do on my explorations and am searching for a new direction. Opportunely, a friend arrives from California to spend a week with me. At this time, a large area of my garden is filled with giant many- petalled red poppies. Sunlight shines through them as they sway and dance in the wind. When she looks at the paintings and also my small flower drawings done with pencil crayons and watercolour paints, she requests I create a picture of these red poppies for her. Great, my next project has arrived. The following week, I take out a full 22" x 30" watercolour sheet and slightly groan. The design of these beautiful poppies is complex and presents a new challenge because they are not as simple as my usual four-petal variety that I am used to depicting. I look at the empty white paper. The paper stares back at me.

Eventually I pick out a few coloured pencils and tentatively develop a variety of layers in a general pattern. These flowers will be much larger than my usual drawings. Additional colours and washes are placed on top of the penciled colours increasing the brilliance. Depth and highlights are added using Chinese watercolours. A bumblebee enlivens the center of one of the poppies and completes the painting. Several days later, I regard the picture with disappointment. It's satisfactory but definitely does not have the energy and exuberance that my friend was wanting.

Putting it aside, I begin a second picture. This time I keep in my mind, not thoughts about the flowers or technique, but thoughts about my friend and her passion for life. I bring that spirit into my body while I paint.

At the end of a week, simply by living the quality my friend exhibits, I gaze at the filled page of much larger poppies that also emit vibrating energy. Additionally, while connecting with my friend, my own enthusiasm has returned. Acting as if I contain her vitality, effected this quality in me. The work is called *Poppies.* (Figure 24)

I am so happy seeing and feeling the returning life energy in these poppies, I do not want to part with them. But my friend has been promised a painting. And so, I begin a third picture that is completed during the next two weeks. I am becoming more confident doing the intricate petal arrangement of ballerina-like poppies blowing in the wind. Also, I have developed ease in using the three mediums together: coloured pencils, watercolour pencils, and Chinese watercolours. Upon completion, these flowers exude vibrant energy and in addition, joy. I believe these poppies best reflect my new energy.

My friend is thrilled when she receives this work. I have regained self-assurance and a sense of positive accomplishment. She asks for framing ideas and I suggest a simple, narrow gold metal frame that will allow the painting to be the main feature. But she decides to use a wide mat and a large gilded gold frame. It will hang over her mantelpiece. I'm surprised but remember this is exactly the reason why I don't want to frame any of my paintings. If I choose a wooden frame, the buyer changes it to a metal frame, or vice versa. After all, most people reason that the frame needs to coordinate with furniture in their room. I let go of any attachment and know the painting will be enjoyed.

More importantly, I have my energy and a desire to paint again.

16. The Child's Gift, Continued

It is now more than two-and-one-half years since beginning this painting of myself as a child. It's the only painting not yet completed, so I return to this picture and my process.

First, I add golden tones to the walls. Face and body flesh colours are strengthened. I change the proportions of hands, arms and legs. As I alter the hair, the head size changes. Very slowly, a newly proportioned and different looking child appears. And yet, she is the same height, and takes up the same canvas space, as did the original image.

The floor is repainted. Adding white and dark tone contrasts on the dress create a more lifelike costume, a more accurate word than outfit as it was in a long-ago period. I add darker colours to her hair and features and emphasize her sparkling blue eyes.

The final challenge in this picture is to complete the ray of light entering the room. Very slowly, using a dry brush technique in which the brush carries a very small amount of paint, I stroke an angle of light down the canvas taking care that it does not become a solid beam.

Over a period of several days, thin strokes of white and intermittent glistening gold paint are alternately added. The light rays gradually emerge in strength. Streaks of the same gold as in the flower and additional solid white are final touches.

Fig. 25 The Child's Gift

This is as much colour as I can safely place in this area in order to give intensity to the stream of light and yet still allow the appearance of glimmering particles. I rename it *The Child's Gift.* (Figure 25)

Comparing snapshots of the first painting and this current one, I see a clear difference between these two children. The latest rendition has more balanced proportions and I appear to be more compact and at ease with my surroundings. My feet are quite solidly placed on the ground. This youngster also seems to reflect something currently of me in my daily life, where I feel better integrated and have more vitality than previously.

While gazing at her face, I notice it appears more adult than her body, for there are no accidents during this series of paintings. Deciding to leave this painting, I mentally note that there is an incomplete adult when my *child's gift* part of me is not honored, or when young sensitivity and pain are not understood.

Trepidation about stepping out into the beam of light shows in my timid glance. The particular reasons for my fear are not clear. Maybe it's not necessary to understand why but only to notice what is and to change my perceptions of what can be, and then act as if it is so. By picturing and believing myself in exactly my desired situation, I can recreate my life. Musing, I observe that this child is not only me but she seems to represent all children. I stand quietly, growing up with myself for company, cared for but not given a great deal of affection. I am not, as is the case with millions of other children in the world, neglected or abused. Looking very cautiously around, I am aware of the light coming into the room and clutch to my breast a very special flower.

This flower is central to the painting. Although very fragile, it feels like it belongs to me. Clutching it tightly, and I am ready to give it to someone but not sure it is an acceptable gift. Gold is the only colour I use here because it is bright and represents both life and spirituality to me.

A few weeks pass and I perceive a more subtle but fuller understanding of what I call the essence of the flower. It is the most important part of me, a very special responsibility inside my being, and has an extremely valuable function that can be nurtured or destroyed. This flower represents my inner spark, a flame of life that is a gift. It represents a quality and direction of life that is my Soul: an energy that needs to be fully expressed. Each of us is born with his/her own flower, a talent to develop. Recognizing and aiding in the expression of the child's inborn desire gives him or her vibrant energy, creates satisfaction and contributes to a successful adult life.

This *me* is the loving, exuberant, excitable, curious, creative, imaginative original child, a blessing, who came onto earth to be welcomed, accepted, loved, guided and encouraged to live her own perfect way of life. This is my possible life. This not only the possibility, but also the need and right, for all children. There is now a cry inside me to release myself, to be free.

Several years have passed and I look back at the inner work involved in creating this picture. The stages of painting *A Child's Gift* illustrated changes in me over time as I released layers of stuck energy that hid an authentic innate child. This child figuratively and literally stood safely in a corner wondering if her gift was acceptable. Trepidation and fear governed her actions, or more often non-actions. The flower, symbolizing Soul essence was alive, held securely and waiting to be given to the world.

As time passed, increased acceptance of this child and myself arrived. Looking at this picture I realized that I, the painter, still looked from above as an observer. I decided that for now the painting was complete.

17. Reflections

Years have passed since I began to write this book. Experiences and time itself contributed to greater self-awareness and understanding of the process of being human. These paintings and inner explorations have had a movement and life of their own. They were unrelentingly compelling me to paint and search various directions, and through many depths of previous unacknowledged pain, to research self-understanding.

In sharing this writing and painting, I feel vulnerable. Although this is a personal search, many other individuals are treading similar paths of discovery and reclaiming their own original inner inheritance. We are like a web connecting to one another and also creating a greater whole as each one builds a section with stronger threads; our humanness becomes more powerful.

Facing a blank canvas at first seemed overwhelming due to my inner expectations followed by fear of failure. Any new project presents either hesitation, or the opposite attitude of stepping right ahead and walking through the challenges. Finally, with persistence a completed project brings varying degrees of satisfaction. It may or may not be appreciated by others, but just trying is a first success, and making a serious effort is a personal gain.

My artwork is usually representational, symbolic and/or metaphorical. As I worked on these paintings, my own hidden inner life became more visible. The unconscious surfaced in the pictures, exposed and ready to be interpreted for additional understanding.

Eventually, thoughts and experiences developed clarity, and words and increased vocabulary became available.

Inner calmness and peace always arrive for me during my creating process and my life itself feels enriched. Many find a sense of self through gardening or other active pursuits. I understand myself through my art. Looking back on these particular pictures, light is thrown on a process of becoming: humanity's path.

When I imagine, feel and act as though a situation is already present, a new reality develops. Imagining helps to focus on a goal, but trouble ensues, and my life and future mature as fantasy, if I simply ponder without taking action. Thoughts and emotions constantly play a powerful role in transforming the quality and opportunities of our lives. Allowing thoughts of worry and fear in the vision defines what will be created. Conversely, action backed by desire, will, happiness and contentment, produces a positive outcome.

When I deny underlying stuck emotions, they remain inside and are often unintentionally projected outward, affecting all in the environment. Our thinking and even illness can affect others. One choice is to remove myself physically from an undesirable environment or individuals. Another position is to learn to emotionally detach. This does not mean to be non-compassionate but to be able to become an interested observer, acting positively and independently from that position.

For myself, when I waken and put a small smile on my face, I feel that smile inside creating a positive environment for myself. There's value to the statement, *be happy*. Understanding human feelings, legitimate and universal, helps to create compassion for others and me. Perhaps this is the *beyond of love* and becomes wisdom and joy.

By taking breaks from regular routines I relax and release, and I create fewer emotional blocks. When I ignore a need for me to change my attitude or actions, stuck energy creates pain. I become numb and inactive, just as a pond is frozen by winter cold. There, when a pebble or small rock is thrown onto the ice it slides uncontrolled and doesn't affect the ice or water beneath. Protecting ourselves by a wall of ice, we avoid being affected by feelings. Any living quality is held inside and it is certainly difficult to control events that run over us. Alternatively, the metaphor of a calm lake is often used to give the idea of tranquil emotions and sometimes, even a serene mind. Thus, I return to the metaphor of a lake compared to human beings. When I throw a pebble into a calm warm summer lake, ripples are created and they move around the lake's surface. The water beneath is also changed. The larger the rock, the greater effect on both the surface and in the depth. Human beings react in the same way as the lake because we are energy, and we are mostly water. Small events create small waves and large events can bring floods or disasters. And in contrast to hiding feelings, similarly, if our minds and emotions become too active, we develop inner and outer chaos.

Inner calmness and peace always arrive while I am creating. Art enriches my life allowing unconscious understanding to surface. I can safely express my deepest emotions. Others find their sense of inner peace through gardening or other creative activities. Creativity is a basis of movement in our lives.

Physics tells us that all molecules are in perpetual motion, even in the chair I sit upon. Cells and organs; everything in my body is in constant transition. Needing movement in our lives, I wonder if this perhaps partially explains why individuals go on cruises? Others derive enjoyment from the speed of a train, a sailboat or even cars. Do these activities supply the gratification of action that may not be present in our daily routines?

Some individuals say that we are always in the perfect place with the exact experience we need. I think at times that may be true, but perhaps it is mainly training for us to discover how best to make choices. We can learn from any experience but as we face many forks in our path some decisions are made with careful judgment and others are randomly or impetuously chosen. I've often hesitated with uncertainty, knowing there was great importance to my decision choosing a direction. Selections are based on experience and knowledge as well as intuitive sensing.

Knowledge of history is helpful to develop options. I think it is even more important for children to learn to examine various alternatives and their possible results. Instead of answers being supplied, a practice of practical participation in analyzing both outcomes and consequences could increase individual and group confidence for choices of clear directions. It could also loosen the bonds of beliefs and open more doors of possibilities. It seems to me that giving children circumstances for learning these processes might eliminate much misery in the world.

Keeping open to new ideas and situations allows possibilities to appear. I also have the freedom to remove myself from negative environments and people. Or I can develop emotional detachment, while at the same time keeping an awareness of people and situations.

Epilogue

There is a saying about every cloud having a silver lining. This thunder cloud I have passed through certainly has had a wonderful lining. I have learned so much about myself and humanity. I feel joy and peace and am free to make my own decisions and choose my own goals. I've made mistakes during my risking to step out into the light and activities. But I feel so much more alive and happy.

I express myself more easily both as to assertiveness and allowing vulnerability.

My quiet voice has greater sound and strength.

Fears are less and I use more flexibility in daily routines.

I can tolerate medium sized risks.

I take events more as they come with less reacting and with clearer evaluating about what is going on.

I don't allow the "sins of the father" to affect my life... it was their beliefs, not necessarily mine.

I am free at last to accept my parents as they were and to allow myself to forget some of their ways.

I can thank them internally for the various strengths they exhibited and from which I learned.

I feel freedom and an ability to change perspective regarding a situation.

I know if I feel "low" that by taking action, especially some creative action, my spirit and outlook will improve.

Setting up fences or boundaries doesn't necessarily mean safety. It curtails my freedom and thus my transformation.

Seeing that life is movement and change creates endless possibilities. Water becomes steam or ice. Fire creates warmth, ashes, and a chance for "Phoenix to rise".

Releasing old patterns, and limitations creates space for new.

I feel lighter physically, emotionally, and mentally.

My mind is more open and less judgmental of myself and others. Therefore I can love myself more which enables me to love others more.

Life is about movement and change. A natural inclination is to retain the status quo, holding on. If I keep clutching onto anything or anyone no longer serving my purpose, my life energy can not only be slowed, but my living quality can be cut off.

Life here on earth is impermanent. In the long run, none of what I've written really matters. Like Ecclesiastes 3:1 "To everything there is a season . . . A time to be born and a time to die." Flowers bloom, send forth their seeds and return to earth. Eventually I will make my transition also.

So, what is important? What is important is how I react to my life and the situations I meet there. Each second contains a seed for the next moment. I'm reminded of a statement that is earliest attributed to Buddha, "Don't just do something, stand there." It suggests stopping or slowing down to take time to relax, and allow a wisdom answer to filter through the silent space. When this happens, I know what is right. This is a wonderful gift.

Our life is a process of *becoming.* We maintain our inner stillness. The ultimate is to *be,* and simply living a quality such as love, or acceptance, or joy, or compassion, or even several positive qualities. To reach a goal of simply to quietly *Be* with inner stillness in each moment.

We are that livingness.

And we continue Being, we create life:

Our life is art.

Postscript

Reflecting on my feeling of relief now that this writing has been finished, I question why I continued this course instead of simply changing direction. Could I have chosen instead to concentrate on creating a new and different reality? The answer is yes, but would I have so clearly understood and accepted myself? I think I gained a fuller picture of my life patterns.

For the past few years, I haven't wanted to hang *The Child's Gift* in my house. The hesitation and trepidation showing in this painting reflected an important quality of fear that I have been trying to understand through my process of painting and writing. In spite of successes in my lifetime, I still questioned my value. This personal need was part of the inner director, driving me forward through my whole process of painting and writing.

Standing still and gazing at this painting one day, I found small tears of sadness surfacing. Surprised, I inwardly felt the reality of my residual pain. Identifying with this so completely meant I could lovingly embrace and assimilate it. In doing so, emptiness disappeared and wholeness developed. Rather than a response to a peripheral awareness, compassion finally reached into the depth of my heart where I experienced a fullness and connection. And finally, I have come to accept and even to love myself. Perhaps a missing, frightened but protected, portion of my Soul has returned to me.

The Child's Gift now hangs in my living room. It feels right in that place.

Hopefully individuals reading this book may be encouraged to begin, or continue more deeply, a journey of personal understanding, thereby achieving their own freedom to create remarkable lives for themselves and their children.

Art As Process

Art is a process
spiraling creation
no visible beginning
no visible end
constant creativity
relentlessly active
begun eons past
moving to future
continually evolving
occasionally stopping
a moment's reflection
thinking it's finished
our thought or thing
captures a moment
in emerging cycles
of endless time

Life is creating
a part of continuum
as through it we join
with Total Creation
thinking through heart
with clear intent
joining with Spirit

as co-Creators
envisioning freely
in a sense of foundation
and state of stability
connecting with Soul

And Art is Life
outcome uncertain
ongoing creating
awareness of Spirit
linking with ground
entwining together
expressing Beauty
eternally present
seen and unseen
becoming visible

And Life is Art

Margaret Braim Little

I Dreamed a Dream

Here is the original dream, written in italics. It contains the words as they appeared to me. I wrote them down as I slowly wakened.

I DREAMED A DREAM (FEB 2, 1993 4:30 AM)

At 4:30 am in 1993 I dreamed a dream that continued from my sleeping state into wakefulness, words pouring through my mind.

Today I reached a turning point. I don't know if now is the exact moment, or if it is only today that I've begun to be aware that I want to burn all the paintings I've done during the past two years. The only thing holding me back is a question of whether, if I keep the paintings, they can help others.

As usual I am beginning my story at the end. I even read newspapers front page first and then I read the back page and then proceed backward from there. So let me now go to . . . I was going to say the beginning, but who ever knows where anything really begins.

Therefore, I'll starts at a point four and one-half years ago, when my partner and husband of thirty-four and one-half years decided to leave and end our relationship.

In retrospect, I realize that our relationship had been dying for many years: inertia, fear, hope of one or both of us changing, and many other factors all entered into the holding on and into the separation. Pain piled upon pain until, along with the inability for clear communications, came frustration and anger in us both. The elastic band finally snapped. As a result of the parting, I went into a major depression-despair, guilt, shame, judgment, anger and the self-questioning of "Why?"

A year earlier we moved from a busy city, a larger family home and our associate network, to a small, rural island and a small, uncared for cottage.

I had lost any desire to paint, so much so that the actual picking up of a paintbrush was impossible. I had turned instead to drawing wild flowers using pencil crayons.

My painting impasse finally broke when I began to express my feelings freely and spontaneously with poster paint on newsprint. This was done with the encouragement of the psychologist.

My so called negative feelings frightened me because part of my upbringing was "don't be cheeky" and "children should be seen and not heard." Old tapes coiled around inside me.

This hurt was too much and the feelings were some I'd been programmed to not even admit having, let alone speak about or show to an outside observer.

Because of my previous experience in painting, I was strongly encouraged to allow myself to acknowledge these feelings on canvas.

Thank you for reading about the story of these paintings.

Margaret Braim Little: February 2, 1993, 4:30 a.m.

About the Author

Margaret Joan Braim Little, born July 1, 1929 in Vancouver, BC, was an only child to Mamie and Jack Braim. Her artistic talents were evident early. She won her first art award at the age of 11 and went on to exhibit and teach art and win further awards into the 1990s.

All through high school she took art classes at UBC. Jack Shadbolt and B.C Binning were two of her most influential instructors at that time.

Art and design school in Ontario called her, but her mother, an award-winning potter, encouraged her to do something "practical" as she knew a career as an artist was a precarious one.

She received a Bachelor of Home Economics from UBC, while taking as many art course as she could. After receiving her BC Teacher's Certificate, Margaret taught Home Economics for three years before leaving to marry and raise two daughters. The family lived in Calgary, Victoria, Winchester (Massachusetts) and London (Ontario) and also spent a year in Lausanne Switzerland.

Margaret continued to make art, pursue art history and technique courses, teach and experiment in numerous mediums. A woman ahead of her times, her work in the 70s explored themes of the environment and nature in particular. Greg Curnoe and Herb Ariss were two highly supportive influences. She also was keenly interested and followed through with in-depth study in Colour Theory and Insight Art Therapy.

In 1987, after moving to Salt Spring Island, she immersed herself in the island's expansive artist community. It was at this time that she began delving more deeply into family dynamics, and her own childhood experiences. This book is a result of that exploration through art therapy and writing.

Walking into her home in Sidney, BC, where she settled in 2002, was like walking into an art gallery with a multitude of different artists. Over her lifetime she worked in oils, acrylics, etchings, pastels, pen and ink and watercolours. As a lover of beautiful fabrics, she learned silkscreen, batik, block print and silk painting. While on Salt Spring Island, she ventured into watercolour pencils. She also hand-built boxes, using book board and covering them with hand-made papers from around the world. Margaret also partook in a Chinese water colour class at University of Western Ontario, and was gifted a special square stamp meaning "beautiful lady", which indeed she was inside and out. In her later years, her creative life turned more towards writing.

Art was Margaret's most powerful way of communicating deeply felt ideas, feelings and beliefs. She processed her life and experiences through her art. Her spiritual life was also important to her, in particular the Ageless Wisdom and Buddhist principles of compassion and loving kindness; and this informed her life and her art.